THIS BOOK BELONGS TO

DEDICATION

This book is for every young person—
and those who are young at heart.
You are a brilliant and engaging rising star.
You are a precious gift to your family and the
world. You carry our history, our dreams, and
our trust.
Know that the world is waiting for your shine.
With love and purpose:

Sam and Rita Burke

I am Brilliant
I see the rising sun's promise!

(So I'll rise!)

I am making history!
I walk with power!

(So I'll rise!)

I am a rising star,
I am a dreamer!
I am unstoppable

(So I'll rise!)

I am one of God's beautiful creations!

(So I'll rise!)

I am claiming
my place to bloom!

(So I'll rise!)

I believe in myself
and my ability to shine

(So I'll rise!)

I look forward
to my journey!
I laugh,
I live,
I love!

(So I'll rise!)

I am Confident
there's no one like me

But still, I promise to like you,
and you, and you

(So I'll rise!)

I am like you, and you, and you!
I live each day with joy!

(So I'll rise!)

I feel special,
I am special
I will always be proud to be me

(So I'll rise!)

When I feel cherished by
family and friends,
I shine brighter
and go further!

(So I'll rise!)

I am my parent's joy,
My teacher's bright student
My caregiver's light.

(So I'll rise!)

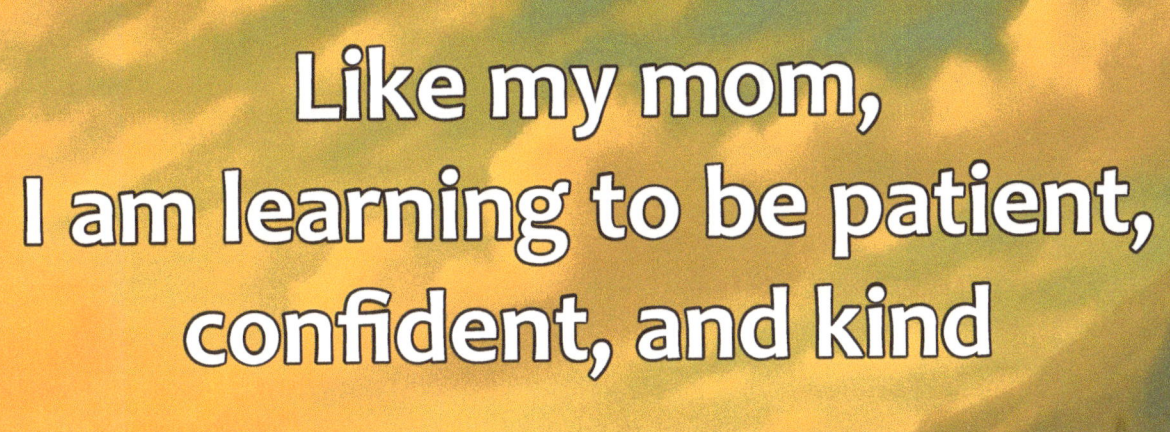

Like my mom,
I am learning to be patient,
confident, and kind

(So I'll rise!)

I believe in myself!
And my ability to shine!

(So I'll rise!)

I am a reader, a writer, a future scientist!

Mom says, " I see something in you! Like Dr. Charles Drew, one day you will rise to greatness"

(So I'll rise!)

ACTIVITY PAGE

Write and / or draw your response to:

I AM- THEREFORE WE ARE

Write:

_____

_____

_____

Draw:

 Sam and Rita Burke have spent over three decades connecting families to books and books to familes through their bookstore. They believe that social and emotional growth flourishes when adults intentionally create the right environment and gift children books as often as possible.

As authors of I Like Being... series, they are dedicated to creating playfully written stories that spark a lifelong love of reading.

An imprint of Burke's Publishing